SECRET

DORSET

BY ROBERT WESTWOOD

Inspiring Places Publishing
2 Down Lodge Close
Alderholt
Fordingbridge
SP6 3JA

www.inspiringplaces.co.uk

ISBN 978-0-9928073-7-5
All rights reserved
© Robert Westwood 2016
Contains Ordnance Survey data © Crown copyright and database right (2011)

Contents

Front cover: The Abbot's Porch, Cerne Abbas.
Back cover: Houns-tout cliff, the Isle of Purbeck.

Introduction

Dorset is a county renowned for its rural beauty and spectacular coastline. It receives many thousands of visitors each year and some of its most popular destinations are known worldwide; but a county with over three and a half thousand miles of 'B' and minor roads and over forty per cent of its landscape a designated Area of Outstanding Natural Beauty is almost inevitably going to have many less well known places to interest the traveller. The aim of this book is to inform visitors to the county of these numerous locations and to provide advice on what to see and details of their often fascinating history, both human and natural. Practical information on how to get there is provided and it is hoped that the many photographs will give you an idea of what delights await should you decide to visit these special places. Many of the locations will, of course, be known to locals of the region, but it is hoped that they too might find something new and interesting to explore. Most places are generally free to enter although churches request a donation and one, Cerne Abbas Abbey, asks a small fee be put in an honesty box. It is possible to combine a visit with a longer walk and the OS Explorer maps OL15, 116, 117 and 118 will be most useful. I should say that these are my personal choices, it is certainly not a definitive list of Dorset's hidden treasures – there are many more for you to discover.

Above: The face of the Cerne Abbas Giant, quite a well known feature, but did you know you can walk on the Giant on one day of the year? - at dawn on May 1st when the Wessex Morris Men perform there.

SHAFTESBURY

Berwick
St John

Ludwell

Stour Row

Guy's
Marsh

Cann

Charlton

Winke

277
Win
Green

Twyford

Cann
Common

Melbury
Abbas

B3081

Tollard
Royal

Compton Abbas

Woo

East
Orchard

Bedchester

7

Fontmell
Magna

Ashmore

CRANBORNE

12

West
Orchard
aston

13

Sutton
Waldron

CHASE

Farnham

nmoon

Iwerne
Minster

122

Stubhampton

Chettle

ld
rd

Fort

6

190

Iwerne Courtney
or Shroton

Tarrant
Gunville

ROMAN

Chettle
House

G
St M

Hambledon
Hill

Shillingstone

143

Pimperne
Down

Tarrant
Hinton

ROAD

10

Long
Criche

Hod
Hill

A350

106

Tarrant
Launceston

Stourpaine

Tarrant
Monkton

Durweston

Pimperne

Blandford
Camp

Mansw

urnworth

**BLANDFORD
FORUM**

Tarrant
Rawston

Bryanston

Blandford
St Mary

Langton
Long Blandford

Tarrant
Keyneston

Tarrant
Rushton

Wi

Winterborne
Stickland

5

B3082

Charlton
Marshall

Tarrant
Crawford

Winterborne
Clenston

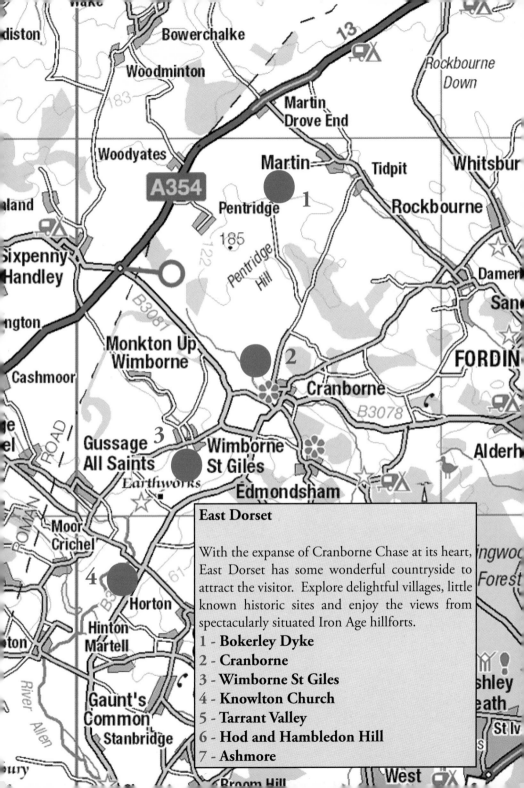

East Dorset

With the expanse of Cranborne Chase at its heart, East Dorset has some wonderful countryside to attract the visitor. Explore delightful villages, little known historic sites and enjoy the views from spectacularly situated Iron Age hillforts.

1 - **Bokerley Dyke**
2 - **Cranborne**
3 - **Wimborne St Giles**
4 - **Knowlton Church**
5 - **Tarrant Valley**
6 - **Hod and Hambledon Hill**
7 - **Ashmore**

Cranborne and surrounding area

Cranborne is a small village on the edge of the 'Chase' to which it gives its name and which came into being as a royal hunting ground. Once a favourite with King John, it developed into an important administrative centre and garrison town. Henry VIII built a hunting lodge which was remodelled in the early seventeenth century by Robert Cecil, 1st Earl of Salisbury, into the beautiful manor house we see today. The manor stands on the site of Cranborne Abbey; founded in the tenth century. It is not open to the public but good views of it are to be had from the B3081 as it leaves Cranborne and particularly from the footpaths bordering the north side of the grounds where a notice charmingly tells visitors they are free to wander over the land and picnic if they wish. On Wednesdays in summer the lovely gardens bordering the manor are open via the garden centre.

On the eastern side of Cranborne, just as the B3078 enters the village, Castle Hill Lane leads up to the site of **Cranborne Castle**. This was a motte and bailey castle, one of many built by the Normans in the years

following the Conquest. Nothing now remains of the building, probably just a wooden structure, but the hill or motte still stands and it is a lovely place to explore, especially in early summer when the bluebells and wild garlic are out.

Cranborne has two pubs and a restaurant plus a tea room at the garden centre. The "Inn at Cranborne" was formerly the "Fleur de Lys" which featured as the "Flower-de-Luce" in Thomas Hardy's *Tess of the d'Urbervilles* and was where, one Saturday night, Tess fatefully accepted a lift home from Alec d'Urberville.

A few miles along the B3078 from Cranborne to Wimborne lies **Knowlton Church**. Many regard this as a special place, a medieval church set inside a Neolithic henge constructed over four thousand years ago. It is a beautiful and atmospheric spot; go late on a summer's evening and you will not be disappointed. There is a parking space outside the henge which is a few yards up a small road, signed Wimborne St Giles and Brockington, between the Horton Inn and the road to Verwood.

Again a few miles out of Cranborne, this time westwards along the B3081, you will find the best preserved Roman road in southern Britain. Just before the roundabout on the A354 you can clearly see the straight bank, known as **Ackling Dyke** stretching away either side of the road. You are free to walk along the Roman road in either direction.

The village of **Wimborne St Giles** is also worth a short visit. The estate here has been in the same family since Norman times. St Giles House was begun in 1650 by Anthony Ashley-Cooper, one of the chief architects

Page 6 top: Cranborne Manor in winter. Page 6 bottom: The motte of Cranborne Castle. Page 7: Knowlton Church.

of the Restoration and made 1st Earl of Shaftesbury by Charles II. The seventh earl, also Anthony Ashley-Cooper was the famous philanthropist and champion of the poor. He campaigned for the abolition of child labour and was one of the founders of Great Ormond Street Hospital. His tomb is in the fine Georgian church, built in 1732. St Giles House is not open to the public but there are several events held there each year, including the now well known Dorset Chilli Festival in August. The quaint alms houses next to the church date from the seventeenth century and by the side of the road nearby are the ancient village stocks.

Top: Ackling Dyke. Bottom left: The village sign at Wimborne St Giles. Bottom right: Stocks at Wimborne St Giles and inside the church.

Practical information

Cranborne is on the B3078 10 miles north of Wimborne. There is a small parking place near Cranborne Castle on Castle Hill Lane at SU 058127, nearest postcode BH21 5QG. Footpaths lead from the village square beside the church to the north of the manor where there are fine views of it. Ackling Dyke can be seen on the B3081 at SU 015163, nearest postcode SP5 5QP. There is a layby nearby.

Knowlton Church is at SU 023102, nearest postcode BH21 5AE.

Wimborne St Giles is about 2 miles south-west of Cranborne. You can park on the road near church, SU 031119, nearest postcode BH21 5LZ.

The Tarrant Valley

The Tarrant is a delightful twelve mile long tributary of the River Stour. A typical Chalk stream, its name derives from the Celtic word meaning "trespasser", presumably because of its frequent deviations from its narrow channel. Along this lovely valley are eight villages all bearing the name of the river and all, apart from Tarrant Launceston, with a pretty, medieval church. There are many footpaths to please walkers and a couple of sites that are worth a visit in their own right. At **Tarrant Rushton** an old airfield has now returned to farmland. This was the place where, on the night of June 5/6th 1944, gliders took off for Normandy to land the first troops in Operation Overlord. There is a simple memorial near the entrance and a huge hangar remains; you can walk along the old perimeter road.

At **Tarrant Crawford** an ancient church is all that remains of a once prosperous Cistercian nunnery. The churchyard is said to hold the grave of Queen Joan of Scotland, daughter of King John and, according to one legend, buried in a gold coffin. It is a charming location and there are some interesting medieval wall paintings in the church.

Practical information

Tarrant Crawford Church is on the minor road between Shapwick and Tarrant Crawford. It is open daily; there is parking nearby, ST 922034, nearest postcode DT11 9HU.

You can park at the entrance to Tarrant Rushton airfield on the minor road from Witchampton to Blandford, ST 950061, nearest postcode DT11 8SB.

Page 9: The perimeter road at Tarrant Rushton airfield and, inset, the memorial at the entrance. Above: Tarrant Crawford Church.

Bokerley Dyke

Bokerley Dyke is a linear earthwork on the Dorset / Hampshire border. Dating from the Bronze Age it was remodelled in around 350 AD, prompting speculation that it formed some sort of defensive line for the Romano-British people against the threat of invasion from the Saxons. It overlooks Martin Down, a remarkable slice of ancient Chalk downland. There are many paths to wander and the setting is superb.

Practical information

Bokerley Dyke can be accessed via a small road from the Hampshire village of Martin. There is ample parking at SU 048190, nearest postcode SP6 3LS.

Ashmore

One of the highest villages in Dorset, Ashmore sits at the north-eastern corner of Cranborne Chase. Such villages, high up on the permeable Chalk, have traditionally had problems with water supply and Ashmore famously retains its "Dew Pond" which only very rarely dries out. The pond is a hollow lined with clay and relies simply on rainwater to keep it replenished. It creates a particularly picturesque centre to this quiet, out of the way settlement. On June 24th, Midsummers Day, Ashmore holds the Filly Loo festival. This started in 1956 and is based on the ancient custom of baking and eating cakes around the pond on the rare occasions when it dried out. Today the festival involves processions and dancing and has become quite a tourist attraction.

Near Ashmore and also on the edge of the Chalk upland is **Compton Abbas Airfield**, perhaps the most picturesque airfield in the country and one which positively encourages visitors to come and enjoy the setting and the comings and goings of the small aircraft. There is a cafe and outside terrace where everyone is welcome and it is a great spot for lunch or afternoon tea.

Above: Martin Down from Bokerley Dyke. Below: Compton Abbas Airfield.

Practical information
Ashmore is near Shaftesbury, easily accessed from the B3081, ST 912178, nearest postcode SP5 5AD. Compton Abbas airfield is at ST 890185, nearest postcode SP5 5AP.

Hod and Hambledon Hill

On the edge of the Chalk escarpment and with wonderful views over the valley of the River Stour, Hambledon and Hod Hill are two spectacular Iron Age hillforts. Both are easily accessed and you are free to wander around. Hambledon was originally the site of a Neolithic causewayed camp and was later developed by Iron Age inhabitants into a stronghold. Their ramparts are particularly impressive on the western side of the hill. During the English Civil War the hill was the scene of confrontation between the Dorset Clubmen, a group of locals fed up with constant war, and the forces

Practical information
There is parking between Hod and Hambledon Hill on a small road off the A350 just a little way south of Iwerne Minster, ST 852112, nearest postcode DT11 8PS. A path leads up Hod Hill from here while just back along the road a path by the side of a house leads up to Hambledon Hill.
Main picture: The view from the top of Hod Hill.
Inset: The ramparts on the west side of Hambledon Hill.

of Parliament. They were quickly dealt with by Oliver Cromwell, who held prisoners overnight in the nearby church at Shroton.

Hod Hill seems to have developed later as an Iron Age hillfort than Hambledon and also has impressive ramparts. The Romans built a fort in the north-western corner after they had captured it. Excavations have shown a concentration of Roman ballista catapult bolts in and around the site of one particular Iron Age hut and it has been speculated that they targeted the home of the local chieftain.

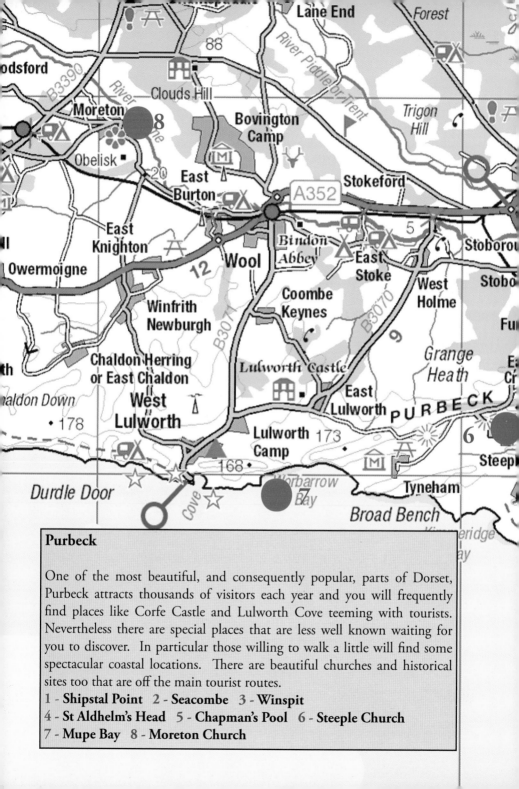

Purbeck

One of the most beautiful, and consequently popular, parts of Dorset, Purbeck attracts thousands of visitors each year and you will frequently find places like Corfe Castle and Lulworth Cove teeming with tourists. Nevertheless there are special places that are less well known waiting for you to discover. In particular those willing to walk a little will find some spectacular coastal locations. There are beautiful churches and historical sites too that are off the main tourist routes.

1 - **Shipstal Point** 2 - **Seacombe** 3 - **Winspit**
4 - **St Aldhelm's Head** 5 - **Chapman's Pool** 6 - **Steeple Church**
7 - **Mupe Bay** 8 - **Moreton Church**

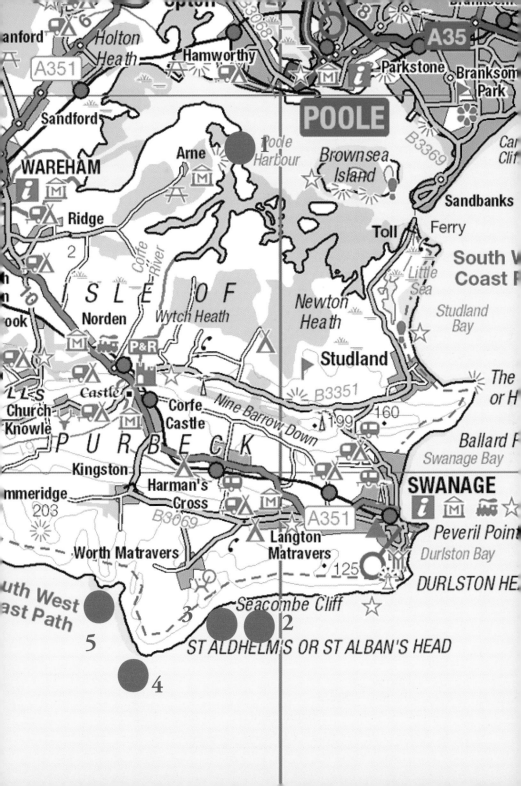

The Purbeck Coast

While Swanage, Kimmeridge, Lulworth and Durdle Door attract thousands of visitors, there are many other beautiful and fascinating places on the coast of Purbeck. While these are not exactly unknown, they are all less frequented and places where you can relax and enjoy the scenery in peace. Typically they require a little effort on foot to get there.

When the army ranges are open the coast path east of Lulworth follows a dramatic course above the famous Fossil Forest before reaching **Mupe Bay**. It is possible to walk/scramble down to the beach and even in the summer you may have it all to yourself. Sometimes you may see a yacht anchored offshore as many sailors know what a beautiful, secluded spot this is.

Picture: Mupe Rocks. Mupe Bay is just around the small headland: the picture is taken from the coast path from Lulworth Cove.

Seacombe.

Many quarries once worked the Portland Stone along Purbeck's southern shore and two of these, **Seacombe** and **Winspit**, are great places to scramble around, sit and relax, and enjoy the sound of the waves on the rocks. Both are easily accessed from Worth Matravers and of the two, Winspit is probably the most well known and attracts most visitors. Winspit was active well into the twentieth century and has vast caves excavated by the quarrymen as well as wonderful views along the Purbeck coast.

Winspit.

Chapman's Pool and Houns-tout cliff.

A shortish, level walk from the small car park on the edge of Kingston will take you to the coast at **Houns-tout**. This high cliff, capped by Portland and Purbeck limestone, provides stunning views east along the Jurassic Coast and west across **Chapman's Pool** and **St Aldhelm's Head**. You can walk down to Chapman's Pool where, again, you may have the beach all to yourself. There is no need to walk back up the steep climb to Houns-tout, you can follow the wooded valley to Hill Bottom and from there take the path to Kingston.

View from St Aldhelm's Head.

St Aldhelm's Head can also be reached from Worth Matravers. Here, again, are wonderful views. There is also a small, Norman chapel dedicated to St Aldhelm, probably on the site of a much older church. The stainless steel sculpture on the headland is a memorial to the development of radar here during the Second World War.

At the other end of Purbeck and on the rim of Poole Harbour is **Shipstal Point**. This is a short walk over the heathland from the RSPB car park at Arne. Another lovely, secluded spot, there is a small sandy beach and the water is almost invariably calm.

Shipstal Point.

Practical information

Mupe Bay is accessed from the coast path east of Lulworth Cove; there is a path up to it from the east side of the cove. It is only accessible when the army ranges are open, that is most weekends and school holidays. See www. dorsetforyou.com/lulworth-range-walks or ring 01929 404819.

Seacombe and Winspit are both reached via footpaths from Worth Matravers where there is a car park, SY 974776, nearest postcode BH19 3LF. The footpath to Winspit starts just below the pond and from there the coast path leads eastwards to Seacombe.

At Kingston carry on up the road past the Scott Arms to find the car park in woods on the left, SY 954795, nearest postcode BH20 5LH.

On the western side of Worth Matravers is another car park at SY 964774, nearest postcode BH19 3LL. From here you can access the coast path and walk down to Chapman's Pool or walk south to St Aldhelm's Head which can also be reached by walking along the track past the car park. There are spectacular views from the coast path.

The RSPB car park, Arne is at SY 972877, nearest postcode BH20 5BJ.

Moreton

A quiet little village at the northern end of Purbeck, Moreton boasts a tranquil setting by the River Frome, a charming tea room, the grave of Lawrence of Arabia and a wonderful church. From the outside you may not think the church of St Nicholas remarkable, but look closely at the windows. The church was unluckily damaged by a stray bomb jettisoned by a returning German bomber in World War II. The building was repaired and the original stained glass windows were replaced by ones engraved by Laurence Whistler. The effect is dramatic and the inside of the church has been transformed. The church held the funeral service of Lawrence of Arabia, whose simple cottage is on nearby Clouds Hill, and his grave is in the "new" churchyard across the road.

Steeple Church

Tucked away in Purbeck's central valley just west of Church Knowle is the tiny village of Steeple; just a few houses and the charming church of St Michael. Carved on the wall of the porch is the coat of arms of the Washington family who had married into the local, wealthy Lawrence family. The first US president, George Washington, was a great grandson of John Washington of Steeple who had moved to Virginia. It is said that George Washington took inspiration for the US flag from the coat of arms on his signet ring which features stars and stripes.

Practical information
Moreton Church is north-west of Wool at SY 805894, nearest postcode DT2 8RJ. Steeple Church is at SY 912809, nearest postcode BH20 5NY. *Middle page: Moreton Church and windows. Above right: Washington arms.*

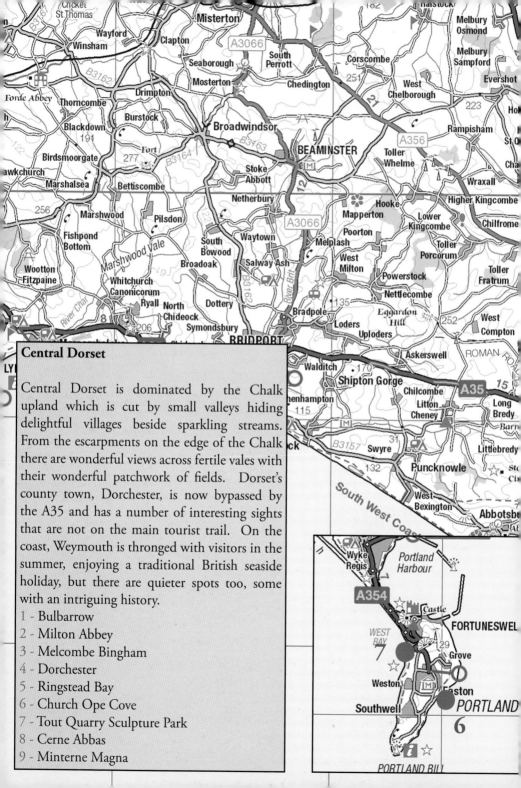

Central Dorset

Central Dorset is dominated by the Chalk upland which is cut by small valleys hiding delightful villages beside sparkling streams. From the escarpments on the edge of the Chalk there are wonderful views across fertile vales with their wonderful patchwork of fields. Dorset's county town, Dorchester, is now bypassed by the A35 and has a number of interesting sights that are not on the main tourist trail. On the coast, Weymouth is thronged with visitors in the summer, enjoying a traditional British seaside holiday, but there are quieter spots too, some with an intriguing history.

1 - Bulbarrow
2 - Milton Abbey
3 - Melcombe Bingham
4 - Dorchester
5 - Ringstead Bay
6 - Church Ope Cove
7 - Tout Quarry Sculpture Park
8 - Cerne Abbas
9 - Minterne Magna

Bulbarrow and surrounding area

Bulbarrow is one of a number of viewpoints on the edge of the Chalk escarpment with views over the Vale of Blackmore, a scene famously described by Thomas Hardy in *Tess of the D'Urbervilles* and in his poem "Wessex Heights". To the north of the road is a small car park with walks around a rare remnant of chalk heathland, again with stunning views and a perfect place for a picnic.

The small intimate valleys that cut the Chalk to the south of Bulbarrow hide a number of "secret" spots that will delight the visitor. The village of **Milton Abbas** is quite well known; it was built in the late eighteenth century by the local landowner who didn't like the proximity to his grand house of

At Bulbarrow.

Milton Abbey from St Catherine's Chapel.

Bingham's Melcombe.

the original village. The long street with its identical thatched cottages is much photographed. Perhaps less visited is **Milton Abbey**; although part of a public school, visitors are welcome to view the abbey and a path leads to St Catherine's Chapel, once reached by a unique line of grass steps. The view from the chapel is lovely.

A little west of Milton Abbas lie the villages of **Lower Ansty** and **Melcombe Bingham** from where a number of relatively short paths lead up to the "**Dorsetshire Gap**", a charmingly named saddle in the Chalk escarpment. Some regard this as the very heart of Dorset and the views certainly reflect the visions of rural beauty and tranquility with which the county is often associated. The even more charmingly named **Bingham's Melcombe** presents a near perfect vision of rural idyll. Although the lovely manor is private, it is possible to walk to the adjacent fourteenth century church of St Andrew, passing the beautiful house on the way.

Practical information

Parking for Bulbarrow at ST 784059, nearest postcode DT11 0HQ. Milton Abbas ST 805017, postcode DT11 0BW and Milton Abbey ST 799024 and postcode DT11 0BZ. The Hambro Arms is a popular pub in Milton Abbas. Lower Ansty, ST 765033, postcode DT2 7PN has the equally popular Fox Inn. You can park on the road near Bingham's Melcombe at ST 773022, postcode DT2 7PZ, and walk to the church. Footpaths lead to the Dorsetshire Gap at ST 743032 from Melcombe Bingham a little way south of the Fox Inn. The OS Outdoor Leisure Map 117 covers this area.

Cerne Abbas

Cerne Abbas lies in a beautiful valley cut into the northern edge of the Chalk downland. This fertile vale has been inhabited since prehistoric times and is in an Area of Outstanding Natural Beauty. The village is well known with many visitors stopping by to see the famous Giant, a 180 feet high figure cut into the hillside and whose age is still debated. Some think it ancient, perhaps representing Hercules since he holds a large club, but there is no mention of it before the seventeenth century and some think it is a caricature of Oliver Cromwell. You may wonder how this famous figure fits in with secret Dorset – well, many visitors fail to find the village's real gems. At the end of the street by the church is Abbey Farm where visitors are allowed (a small donation is requested) to view the remains of the Benedictine abbey which was founded in 987 AD. The remains are meagre but charming; both the **Abbot's Porch** and the **Guesthouse** date from the

The Guesthouse, Cerne Abbey.

fifteenth century. Nearby is a peaceful churchyard with, at the far corner, the **Silver Well**. This lovely spot is a Chalk spring and is reputedly the spot where St Augustine struck the ground with his staff after asking local shepherds if their thirst would be better quenched by beer or water. The spring flowed as a response to their pious reply. However, it owes its name to the more likely and charming story that it is the place where St Edwold, a Saxon nobleman tired of constant warfare, lived as a hermit. He asked the locals where to find water and rewarded them with silver coins when they showed him the spring. Dipping a new born baby as the first rays of the sun strike the water is said to bring health and happiness.

Head north from Cerne Abbas along the A352 and you will shortly reach the little village of **Minterne Magna**. Here is the imposing home of the Churchill and Digby families with gardens open to the public and especially beautiful in May when the azaleas and rhododendrons are out. Just north of the village a road to the left leads along the top of the Chalk escarpment with, after a while, wonderful views over the Vale of Blackmore, Thomas Hardy's "Vale of Little Dairies". By the side of the road is a small enigmatic stone pillar, known as the "**Cross in Hand**". This may have been an ancient boundary marker but in his poem "The Lost Pyx" Thomas Hardy recounts a more interesting origin. Journeying to deliver the last rites to an old shepherd on a stormy night, the local priest lost the silver box (pyx) that held the sacrament. Searching for it, he found the pyx illuminated and with a group of cattle around it. He erected the pillar to mark the spot. It was also the scene in *Tess of the D'Urbervilles* where Alec met Tess and begged her not to tempt him again.

Practical information

Cerne Abbas abbey is at the end of the road past the parish church, at ST 666016, nearest postcode DT2 7GY. The Silver Well is nearby at the end of the churchyard. Minterne Gardens are at ST 661043, postcode DT2 7AU. The Cross in Hand is to be found at ST 633038 (enclosed by fencing at the side of the road), nearest postcode DT2 7BE.

Pages 26, 27: The Guesthouse, Cerne Abbey. Page 28: The Silver Well. Left: The Cross in Hand.

Dorchester

Dorchester is a thriving county town with interesting museums, boutique shops and vibrant bars and bistros. Many, though, will miss some of its fascinating and atmospheric corners. The River Frome skirts its northern edge and the footpath here passes "**Hangman's Cottage**". The name is still on the door of this quaint, private, thatched dwelling and it was formerly the home of the nearby jail's official hangman. If you walked here you probably passed the old jail outside of which sixteen year old Thomas Hardy witnessed the public execution of Martha Brown, reputedly providing the inspiration for the ending of the eponymous heroine of *Tess of the D'Urbervilles*.

A little further on beside the council buildings is the **Roman townhouse** whose expert excavation has revealed a sophisticated ancient home with some beautifully preserved mosaics. Continuing the Roman theme is **Maumbury Rings**, due south and next to Dorchester South station. This was a Neolithic site that became a Roman amphitheatre.

Finally, at the north-western edge of the town on Poundbury Road is **Poundbury hillfort**. This is a lovely spot to wander around and the ramparts of the Iron Age hillfort are still impressive. On the northern side of the hill it is possible to see the course of the Roman aqueduct which was a remarkable piece of engineering built to provide the town with water.

Practical information

The Roman townhouse (above) is in the grounds of County Hall at SY 690909, postcode DT1 1XJ. Hangman's Cottage is just across the road by the river at SY 692910, postcode DT1 1YB. Maumbury Rings is at SY 690899, postcode DT1 1QZ and Poundbury hillfort at SY 681910, postcode DT1 2PN.

Ringstead and White Nothe

White Nothe arguably offers the best views anywhere on the Jurassic Coast. Eastwards you look across the Chalk cliffs to Bat's Head with the limestone headland of St Aldhelm's in the distance, while westwards Ringstead Bay, Osmington Mills, Weymouth and the Isle of Portland stretch before you. You can reach White Nothe from the National Trust Ringstead car park, a short, easy walk of about twenty minutes. Near the headland is a row of isolated cottages, once Coastguard cottages from the days when their job was primarily to catch and deter smugglers. A steep, windy track, signed the "Smugglers' Path" leads down to the shore from the top of the cliff and featured in J. Meade Faulkner's *Moonfleet*.

Practical information

The National Trust Ringstead car park is at SY 758825, nearest postcode DT2 8NQ. From here follow the footpath eastwards to White Nothe.

Above: East from White Nothe. Left: Looking west.

The Isle of Portland

The people of Portland have traditionally considered themselves different from the rest of Dorset. Tenuously connected to the "mainland" by Chesil Beach, Portland does feel to have a character all its own. Thomas Hardy called it the "Isle of Slingers", a reference to the fact that the ancient Celts used the smooth, rounded pebbles from Chesil Beach as ideal ammunition for their slings. Portland, of course, is famous for its stone, a hard Jurassic limestone that is perfect for monumental structures. It has been quarried since Roman times and is still in demand, although most of the quarries are no longer worked. Unlike its near neighbour Weymouth, Portland is not a major tourist destination but Portland Bill with its lighthouse still draws many visitors. There are, however, one or two places that fit perfectly with the aims of this book. **Church Ope Cove** sits midway down the east coast

of the isle just south of Easton and is reached via a steep line of steps from a path by the charming Portland Museum. Guarding it are the ruins of Rufus Castle, reputedly built for William Rufus (William II) although the present structure dates from the fifteenth century. Also overlooking the cove and reached by a short path are the ruins of St Andrew's Church. This was the first parish church on Portland and was the site of an early Saxon church. It was abandoned in the eighteenth century after a landslip made it unsafe. It is now a lovely spot with fine views out to sea. In the graveyard is a very unusual gravestone; instead of a cross the emblem it carries is a skull and crossbones. In fact several tombs and graves have this design but, perhaps disappointingly, it does not mean pirates were buried here, it was simply used to represent man's mortality.

Church Ope Cove itself has a rocky, pebbly beach and is one of the few places on Portland where it is safe and easy to swim off, although only within the cove. There is a lovely coastal path to the south leading to Portland Bill.

Some of Portland's quarries offer opportunities to walk and explore. In particular **Tout Quarry Sculpture Park** in the north-west corner of the isle has many sculptures in its meandering forty acre site as well as great views over Chesil Beach and the Jurassic Coast.

Practical information
The path to Church Ope Cove starts by Portland Museum at SY 698711, postcode DT5 1HS. Tout Quarry Sculpture Park is off Wide Street, Portland at SY 686727, nearest postcode DT5 2AF.
Page 32 top: St Andrew's Church and churchyard. Bottom: Church Ope Cove.
Page 33 above: Tout Quarry Sculpture Park.

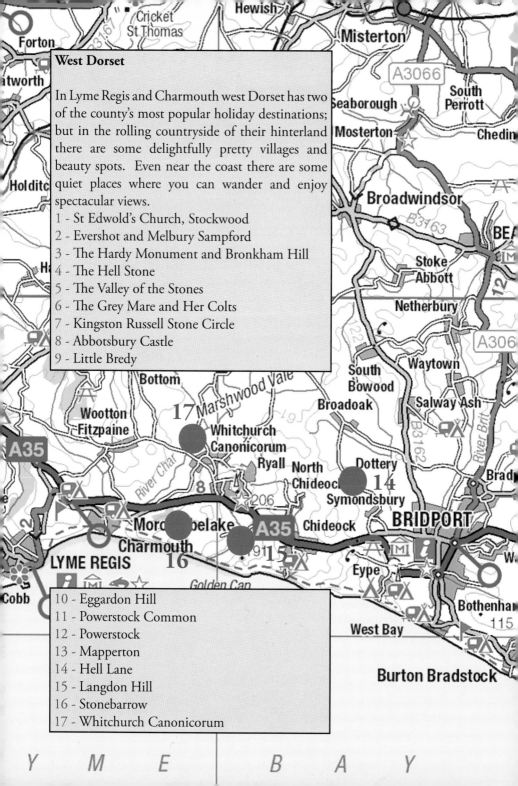

West Dorset

In Lyme Regis and Charmouth west Dorset has two of the county's most popular holiday destinations; but in the rolling countryside of their hinterland there are some delightfully pretty villages and beauty spots. Even near the coast there are some quiet places where you can wander and enjoy spectacular views.

1 - St Edwold's Church, Stockwood
2 - Evershot and Melbury Sampford
3 - The Hardy Monument and Bronkham Hill
4 - The Hell Stone
5 - The Valley of the Stones
6 - The Grey Mare and Her Colts
7 - Kingston Russell Stone Circle
8 - Abbotsbury Castle
9 - Little Bredy

10 - Eggardon Hill
11 - Powerstock Common
12 - Powerstock
13 - Mapperton
14 - Hell Lane
15 - Langdon Hill
16 - Stonebarrow
17 - Whitchurch Canonicorum

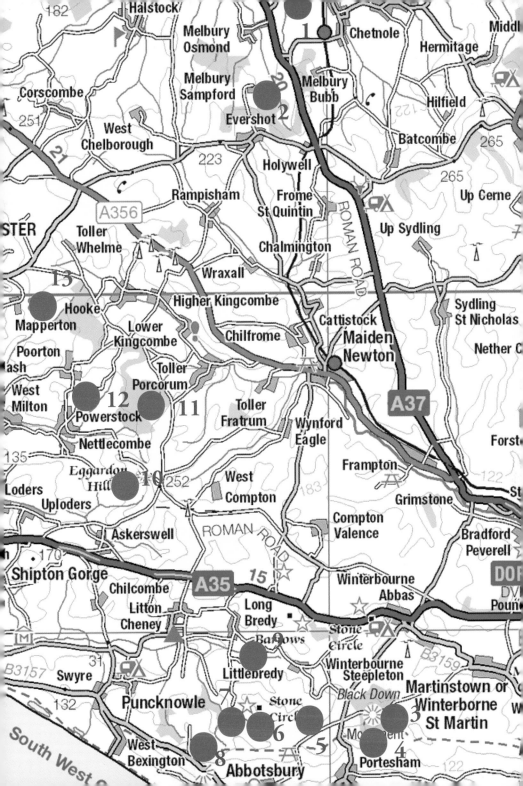

The Hardy Monument and surrounding area

The Hardy Monument was built to honour Dorset's other Thomas Hardy, the naval hero who was Nelson's Flag Captain at Trafalgar. He was born in the nearby village of Portesham. The views are impressive and the monument served as a marker for shipping off Weymouth; its shape was intended to mimic a naval telescope. Just to the south-east of the monument is **Bronkham Hill**, along which the South Dorset Ridgeway runs. A walk along here is well worthwhile, the surrounding countryside is lovely and the ridge has many Bronze Age burial barrows.

A short distance west of the Hardy Monument is a little known National Nature Reserve, **The Valley of the Stones**. The name derives from the fact that the valley floor is littered with rocks and boulders of sarsen stone, a very hard sandstone bound by a silica cement. It is thought the rock was broken up by freeze/thaw weathering during the Ice Age and slumped downhill on the frozen subsoil. The rocks were used by Neolithic and Bronze Age people to build stone circles such as the nearby **Kingston Russell** circle. The nature reserve forms the head of the valley of the River Bredy, although the river now starts some way below. It is a charming valley with the village of **Little Bredy** at its heart. The river starts here at a lake artificially created next to Bridehead House. The village is essentially a Victorian estate village built around the manor which was also extensively altered in Victorian times. Next to the lake is a lovely park where you are free to wander and picnic; there is even a waterfall at the end of the lake.

This part of Dorset has many ancient remains from Neolithic times and the Bronze Age; Bronkham Hill mentioned above has numerous burial barrows and there are also stone circles, standing stones and chambered tombs. Several pretty valleys cut the Chalk downs while footpaths along the spurs offer stunning views. One such path offers the chance to see **The Grey Mare and Her Colts**, a chambered Neolithic long barrow and the Kingston Russell Stone Circle. The South Dorset Ridgeway continues west of the Hardy Monument and passes near the **Hell Stone**, another long barrow and eventually reaches **Abbotsbury Castle**, an impressive Iron Age hillfort with lovely views over Chesil Beach and the Fleet.

Practical information

The Hardy Monument is looked after by the National Trust and offers a free car park at SY 613876, nearest postcode DT2 9HY. Parking for the Valley of the Stones is at SY 601874, nearest postcode DT2 9HX. The Kingston Russell Stone Circle is at SY 578878 by the footpath over Tenants Hill while the Grey Mare is at SY 584871 in the corner of a field just off the same footpath. You will probably need OS Explorer Map OL15 to help find this. Parking for both is at SY 589868, nearest postcode DT3 4HA. The park at Little Bredy is at SY 589888, nearest postcode DT2 9JA. The Hell Stone is at SY 605867, just off a footpath which is accessed from the road at SY 601869, nearest postcode DT3 4EY; again OS map OL15 would be useful.

Parking for Abbotsbury Castle is at SY 553864, nearest postcode DT3 4JY.

Page 36: The Valley of the Stones. Above: The park at Little Bredy.

Melbury Sampford, Evershot and St Edwold's Church, Stockwood

Evershot is a lovely village with many fine buildings. Fans of Thomas Hardy will know it as Evershead, the village where Tess stayed on her way back from seeing Angel Clare's parents (*Tess of the D'Urbervilles*). The Acorn Inn features in several books as the "Sow and Acorn", while just up the road from it is Tess Cottage where the eponymous heroine supposedly stayed the night. On the edge of the village is Melbury Sampford, unusual in that a footpath leads through the lovely landscaped grounds and past the imposing Melbury House, owned by Ilchester Estates which also owns much of Abbotsbury.

The little hamlet of Stockwood lies in a charming valley near the village of Chetnole and is home to Dorset's smallest church, and the only one dedicated to St Edwold. No longer in use it is still consecrated and looked after by The Churches Conservation Trust. It seems to belong to the adjacent farmhouse but you are welcome to visit. The church dates from the fifteenth century but since St Edwold was a Saxon saint it probably replaced a much older church. In fact Edwold was the hermit from the Silver Well at Cerne Abbas (see page 29) and probably had a cell here too.

Practical information

It is usually possible to park on the road at ST 576048 nearest postcode DT2 0JZ. This is near the entrance to Melbury Sampford estate through which the footpath leads. Tess Cottage is on the main street just uphill from the church. St Edwold's Church at Stockwood is at ST 590069, postcode DT2 0NG. You can park on the small road leading to it.

Page 38 top: The park at Melbury Sampford.

Page 38 bottom: Tess Cottage, Evershot.

This page (both): St Edwold's Church.

Powerstock, Eggardon Hill and Whitchurch Canonicorum

Powerstock is a small, quaint village a few miles north-east of Bridport. It sits in the steep valley of the Mangerton River and has many pretty cottages, a good pub and a lovely church. This is a beautiful area, just on the edge of the Chalk downs. A little way south-east of the village and carved into the downs, sits Eggardon Hill, another Iron Age hillfort with a magnificent setting. The famous smuggler, Isaac Gulliver, bought a farm here and planted trees on the hill to guide his ships. Eggardon has a number of mysterious legends associated with it including demons, witches and fairies.

Just east of Powerstock and north of Eggardon Hill is **Powerstock Common**, a nature reserve looked after by the Dorset Wildlife Trust. This is an enchanting mix of woodland and grassland with numerous trails to follow. There are many rare and protected species; in spring and early summer there is an abundance of wild flowers while autumn brings fruits and fungi.

Whitchurch Canonicorum is a lovley village in the Marshwood Vale and about five miles west of Bridport. It owes its unusual name to Saint Wite (latinised to Saint Candida) whose remains lie in the church. Apart from Westminster Abbey, where the bones of Saint Edward the Confessor lie, this is the only church in Britain with the remains of a saint. Little is known about St Wite, she may have been a Saxon holy woman murdered by marauding Danes, or possibly an anchoress, a type of religious hermit attached to a particular place. A casket inside her shrine in the church is inscribed with words which translate to "Here rest the remains of Saint Wite" and was found to contain the bones of a woman about forty years old. Today the shrine holds many cards asking the saint for help in healing the sick and injured. The church is known as the "Cathedral of the Vale" and was once a place of pilgrimage second only to Canterbury Cathedral.

Practical information

Powerstock is at SY 517962, nearest postcode DT6 3TD. Parking for Powerstock Common is at SY 547974, nearest postcode DT2 0EJ. The church at Whitchurch Canonicorum is at SY 397954, postcode DT6 6RJ. *Page 40: Eggardon Hill. Page 41 top: The church of St Candida and St Cross at Whitchurch Canonicorum. Below left: St Candida's shrine and right: a figure of St Candida on the south wall of the church.*

Stonebarrow Hill, Langdon Hill and Hell Lane

Charmouth, just to the east of Lyme Regis, is a popular place to go fossil hunting and the Heritage Centre there organise walks with experts to show you how and where to look. However, if you simply want to enjoy the beautiful coastal scenery in a quiet setting with opportunity to walk the dog, picnic or just sit and relax, then head up to Stonebarrow Hill. At the very eastern end of Charmouth narrow Stonebarrow Lane leads to the large National Trust car park from where there are a variety of lovely walks with far reaching views over the Jurassic Coast. Why not follow the path down to the tiny ruined St Gabriel's Church which once served the now vanished village of Stanton St Gabriel. All that remains is the farmhouse, converted to holiday cottages by the National Trust. From here the energetic can walk up to the summit of Golden Cap and enjoy the spectacular views.

Another lovely and secluded National Trust car park can be found on Langdon Hill, just off the A35 between Chideock and Charmouth where a relatively flat walk circles the hill offering wonderful views over coast and countryside as it does so. Like Stonebarrow, this is part of the National Trust's Golden Cap Estate, and again offers a route to the summit of the south coast's highest cliff.

A very different sort of location is situated just north of Chideock; this is Hell Lane, a sunken lane or "holloway". These features were once ancient cattle droves or perhaps pilgrimage routes and centuries of passing carts and cattle has worn into the soft bedrock, in this case sandstone, and created a miniature gorge. It has a wonderfully atmospheric, somewhat mysterious character and walking along it proves a memorable experience – but dry weather is preferable as part of it becomes a watercourse in wet conditions. It is best accessed from the pretty village of Symondsbury where cottages, church and manor are built of the local, golden limestone.

Practical information

The car park at Stonebarrow is at SY 382933, nearest postcode DT6 6SD. Langdon Hill car park is at SY 413931, postcode DT6 6EP and Hell Lane is accessed via the path leading from the road by the side of Symondsbury Church and the manor. You can park on the road at SY 444936, postcode DT6 6HD.

Page 42: Stonebarrow Hill; Golden Cap is in the distance. This page top: Hell Lane. Bottom left: Mushrooms in Hell Lane: Bottom right: Langdon Hill.

Mapperton

Largely dating from the sixteenth century, Mapperton House near Beaminster is another built of golden coloured limestone. Its size is perfect for the intimacy of its surroundings and the unusual Italianate garden behind adds to its charm. It seems lost in the rolling hills of north Dorset and was considered the ideal site for Bathsheba Everdene's farm in the recent Hollywood adaptation of Thomas Hardy's *Far from the Madding Crowd*. It is one of the few places in this book which requires an entrance fee but it is well worth it. You can simply choose to visit the garden or take a tour of the house as well. However, there is no fee to park and enjoy the cafe from where there is a good view of the house and its setting.

Practical information

Mapperton is just off the B3163 east of Beaminster, at SY 503996, postcode DT8 3NR. Check website for opening times, but primarily from March to October except Saturdays.

Top and bottom: The house and gardens.